AF480635

The Sovereign Cat

The Sovereign Cat: A Biographical Poetry Collection.

H. C. CISNEROS

The Sovereign Cat

Copyright © 2026 by *H. C. Cisneros*

Published by Eta Books La Puente, California

LCCN: 2026908478

Website: etabook.com

ISBN: 979-8-9955290-0-2

First Edition: 2026

Printed in the United States of America

CIP DATA

Publisher's Cataloging-in-Publication Data

Names: Cisneros, Herlinda C., author.

Title: The Sovereign Cat : a biographical poetry collection / by H. C. Cisneros.

Description: La Puente, CA: Eta Books, 2026.

Identifiers: LCCN: 2026908478 | ISBN: 979-8-9955290-0-2 (hardcover) | 979-8-9955290-1-9 (paperback) | 979-8-9955290-2-6 (ebook)

Subjects: LCSH American poetry--21st century. | Cisneros, Herlinda C. | Sisters--Poetry. | Sisters--United States--Biography. | Los Angeles (Calif.)--Poetry. | Los Angeles (Calif.)--Biography. | BISAC POETRY / Subjects & Themes / Family | BIOGRAPHY & AUTOBIOGRAPHY / Memoirs

Classification: LCC PS3603 .I76 S68 2026 | DDC 811.6--dc23

Acknowledgments

To God—
For saving me in all forms. For allowing my "test" to become my testimony.

To Muffin—
Thank you for always standing by my side. Through it all—and the many times we fell—you protected our love. To infinity and beyond.

To my children—
You three are my blessing, my pride, and my joy. It is an honor to be loved by you. Remember, the world is at your feet. God will guide you to be anything you want to be—it's really that easy.

Dedication

For Allie—
My protector, my enemy, and my everything.
We loved and bickered with equal weight, but we never let go.
Standing together when the world walked away.
Allie-nese.
The translation of us.
— Erlin

CONTENTS

HOME

SURGE

ADRIFT

KIN

Sovereign (noun) /ˈsäv(ə)rən/

1. A ruler possessing absolute power over their own domain, independent of external interference or outside control. A leader who establishes order where there is chaos and carries the inescapable weight of final authority.

Cat (noun) /kat/

1. A professional stinker who ignores every rule except their own. Known for the "zoomies" at 3:00 AM and staring at blank walls with a look of pure judgment.

HOME

THE BROWN VAN

A dusty sunbeam, a rusty seat,
A tiny bundle, small and sweet.
Only a few months, barely awake,
Inside the brown van that the shadows take.

But there you are, with arms so tight,
Holding me fast, keeping me right.
A click of the camera, a flash in the gloom,
Filling with love that old, brown room.

We grew in the quiet, you and me,
Beside the wheel, a faded memory.
Before I knew the world, I knew your hand,
A sister's love, the safest land.

Years have passed, the van is gone,
But in that picture, we live on.
A snapshot held in my mind so clear,
My first, best friend, who kept me near.

SACRED DOOR

I stood at the threshold, a trespasser small,
Before the great mystery behind her wall.
A room filled with secrets, with shadows and light,
A kingdom forbidden, hidden from sight.

To me, she was legend, the coolest of all,
With posters and treasures pinned to the wall.
I'd tiptoe through the doorway, my breath held in tight,
In awe of the marvels that shone in the light.

Each bottle of cologne, each bauble and ring,
To my five-year-old eyes was a magical thing.
It smelled like adventure, like growing up fast,
A gallery of wonders I hoped would always last.

She was the leader, the one with the key,
To a world that felt miles and miles from me.
Mysterious and bold, in her sovereign space,
I was just a small shadow in her sacred place.

But even back then, in that glow and that grace,
I just wanted to be near her, and see her cool face.
The older sister I worshipped, so wild and so free,
Who let me glimpse the person she wanted to be.

FLIGHT

The shadows were long on the basketball court,
Where the hoop hung in silence, a giant at sport.
I was small in the darkness, a child of six,
Lost in a world that only sisters could fix.

We were walking the concrete, the air growing chill,
When a murmur of danger, silent and still,
I felt the shift in her hand, in her heart,
As the world that felt safe began pulling apart.

"They're coming," someone whispered, a ghost in the ear,
And for the first time, I tasted her fear.
But she didn't falter, she didn't let go,
She didn't let the panic or the terror show.

She gripped my small fingers, she started to run,
Before the first shadow of trouble begun.
We moved like a bolt, like a streak through the night,
Fueled by the surge of the danger that might.

And suddenly, the pavement was no longer there,
I was lifted and carried through the cooling night air.
My feet didn't touch, I was weightless and free,
A bird in the wind that she'd captured for me.

I wasn't running, I was taking to flight,
A tiny passenger in her desperate might.
She ran for our lives, the quickest she's ever sped,
With the sound of my heartbeat inside of my head.

I don't remember the ending, or where we arrived,
Only the relief of having survived.
Beyond the gang members, beyond the dark wall,
She was the wings that wouldn't let me fall.

A sister who flew when the world tried to chase—
The fastest, most beautiful miracle of pace.

WEIGHT OF A NICKEL

I ran to her with a heavy heart and a story of a debt,
A childhood slight, a tiny loss, I haven't forgotten yet.
It wasn't for the money, but for the feeling of the sting,
To a little kid, a missing coin is such a massive thing.

I told her I'd been cheated, that the neighbors weren't fair,
And she didn't stop to question, she didn't even care
If the math was slightly off or if the "crime" was truly real,
She only saw the sadness that her sibling had to feel.

She didn't use a lecture, and she didn't use a plea,
She simply stepped into the role of who she had to be.
A shadow on their doorstep, a presence cold and tall,
Demanding back the justice for a person rather small.

I remember their apologies, the way they bowed their heads,
While I stood safely in the wake of the quiet words she said.
Years have passed and now I know the nickel wasn't the prize,
It was seeing my protector through a younger sibling's eyes.

She gave me back my "fortune," but she gave me something more:
The knowledge that I'd never have to fight a lonely war.
Though I feel a little sorry for the neighbors and their fright,
I'll never lose the feeling of her standing for my right.

STATUES

After three sons, she was the first girl of dawn,
A daughter the house had been waiting upon.
While Dad saw the fire and the rebellion and pride,
Mom saw the beauty and the magic inside.

She didn't use anger, she didn't use fear,
She just kept her precious one forever quite near.
She'd come to the doorway with something wrapped tight,
A gift for the girl who had stayed out all night.

Not a lecture or lesson, or words of despair,
But a horse carved of marble with dust in its hair.
Statues of horses with manes flowing back,
Frozen in mid-air on a permanent track.

Some were of jade and some carved from the rock,
A silent, stone herd that the world couldn't mock.
I remember the shelf where the herd used to stand,
Placed there so gently by our mother's hand.

In a house full of fighting and bottles and noise,
Those horses were anchors of beauty and poise.
Cool to the touch, and so heavy and deep,
A stable of spirits that were hers now to keep.

They were Mom's way of saying, without any word,
That the beauty in Allie would never be blurred.
A quiet Cat with a herd made of stone—
The most cherished daughter that Mom had ever known.

SHIELD

The roar would start before she came in view,
A streak of red that split the morning dew.
On two wheels, she was queen of every street,
With leather boots and pride that couldn't be beat.

She wore that jacket like a coat of mail,
A shield against the world, she'd never fail.
A quiet kind of grace, a hidden, steady heart,
She was scary to the crowd, but kind in every part.

She'd test the threshold first, with a serious, deep stare,
Before she let you in to breathe her private air.
Tough as the asphalt, steady as the steel,
She carried her own strength, and made it real.

I'd watch her kick the stand and kill the light,
A silhouette of power, a glorious sight.
She liked being seen as hard, as fierce, as bold,
With a heart of iron and a story untold.

She was the engine's hum, the highway's song,
The one who taught me how to be just as strong.
Beneath the leather and the "tough woman" pride,
It was the same sister who took me for that first ride.

DIAL

The speakers shook the drywall with a heavy, metal scream,
In a room of dimly lit candles and a Sovereign's dream.
She was a vision in her jacket, with hair feathered and high,
A rock-and-roll disciple under a suburban sky.

From the bite of Ozzy's laughter to the anthem of Whitesnake,
She lived within the volume and the noise that she could make.
She'd headbang to the rhythm, she'd let the power chord roll,
Letting the static of Quiet Riot soothe her restless soul.

But then the dial would wander, and the air would start to change,
To a sound that felt so different, so lonesome and so strange.
She'd twist the knob with a searchful, dedicated hand,
To bridge the heavy metal with the country in the land.

The twang of a guitar string and a story slow and sad,
Finding beauty in the country and the heartaches that they had.
It was a puzzle I would watch, a secret she would keep—
How the music could be jagged, then suddenly be deep.

The rocker and the drifter, both living in one heart,
Two different kinds of loneliness, worlds and worlds apart.
She'd check her hair in mirrors, perfecting every strand,
A sister's kind of armor, held within her command.

With a country song to follow and the metal for the soul,
She'd listen with all her heart to finally fill the hole.

THE WHISTLE

She roamed the streets with a restless heart,
Highly independent, right from the start.
A spirit that couldn't be fenced or tied,
With worlds to discover and nowhere to hide.

But whenever she wanted to find her way back,
Or knew we were searching along the track,
She'd halt in her path where the sidewalk ends,
And call out a signal to family and friends.

With fingers to lips, she'd fill up the space,
A sound so alive it could quicken our pace.
A whistle so sharp, so steady and loud,
It pierced through the traffic and over the crowd.

Blocks away, we would hear that high note,
The sound of a sister, a song from her throat.
Mom in the driver's seat, worried and tense,
Until that familiar sound cleared the fence.

She'd see us first from some corner or hill,
And let out that trill that haunts me still.
She was never lost, she was just being free,
Waiting for us to find her—and her to find me.

CRACKED

The rain was a curtain, thick and gray,
On a road they traveled on a fateful day.
A promise of dinner, a warm, bright light,
Shattered in seconds by a sudden fright.

A roar of metal, a slide on the street,
Where the steel and the water and terror all meet.
They told of the windshield, once clear and so plain,
Spiderwebbed outward from the force of the strain.

No seatbelt to hold her, no warning to stay,
Her head hit the glass in a sickening way.
And then, for a moment, the world was a screen,
Lost in the sirens and the dark in between.

I wasn't there to see the glass, a child of nine,
But I traced the story through every jagged line.
I was certain the heavens had snatched her away,
That the miracle hadn't held on that terrible day.

The crack was a map of the fear in my head:
The "what if" she'd flown—the "what if" she was dead.
But years later, sitting and sharing the past,
She'd let out a laugh that was hearty and fast.

She'd joke of the impact, the strength of the blow,
The girl who broke windows and had nowhere to go.
To her, it was power, just a story to tell,
A sister who tripped but who never quite fell.

But I'd look at her then, with the light on her face,
And see the true work of a silent kind of grace.
She stayed in the seat, she didn't fly to the street,
The miracle kept her world whole and complete.

SPLIT

The walls were thin and the air was strange,
In a place where everything started to change.
A shelter for women, a refuge of sorts,
Away from the fighting and the loud retorts.

Mom brought us there to find some peace,
Hoping the echoes of anger would cease.
But Allie was restless, a cat in a cage,
Her heart full of fire and a teenager's rage.

She stayed for a moment, a day or maybe three,
But she couldn't inhabit that shared misery.
She slipped through the door while the hallway was dim,
Choosing the house and the shadow of him.

I stayed with our mother, a child in the dark,
While Allie went back to leave her own mark.
I heard she was there, in the home we had fled,
With the ghost of the bottles and the words that he said.

She chose the familiar, the hardship, and pain,
While we waited for sunlight to break through the gray.
It's been forty years since that house was so torn,
Since the sister left us to feel so forlorn.

But the miracle happened—the bottle went dry,
And the father we feared learned to look us in the eye.
She went back to find him, and he found his way,
To the honor that keeps them both standing today.

MIRROR

He looked at her face and saw shadows of old,
Of a family he'd left in the dark and the cold.
He'd fought tooth and nail to build something new,
But in Allie, he saw all the ghosts he once knew.

The rebellion, the streets, the wildness of soul—
He tried to break what he couldn't control.
"A child of the streets," was the name that he gave,
As he tried, in his way, to be someone to save.

But his hands were too heavy, his anger too loud,
Like a storm that was trapped in a permanent cloud.
She carried the bruises, the sting, and the debt,
And a lifetime of anger she couldn't forget.

"He's *your* father," she'd tell me, her voice like a blade,
Drawing a line in the choices they'd made.
She didn't want him at the end of the road,
For the weight of the years and the anger she stowed.

Yet beneath the resentment, the fire, and the pride,
Was a daughter who couldn't quite leave his side.
For when he grew weary and the illness took hold,
His *Alejandrita* returned to the fold.

She reached through the decades of silence and pain,
To wash away years of the sorrow and stain.
The man who had hit her, the girl who had fled,
Found a quiet forgiveness in the words left unsaid.

He loved her with fear, and she loved him with grit,
Two sides of a fire that neither could quit.
She was the mirror of all he had feared,
But the one who stood by when the ending appeared.

PROVEN

They called it the place for the restless and wild,
The school for the rebel, the "difficult" child.
With a history of fights and a fire in her eye,
She walked through those doors with her head held high.

She was the outlier, the one they couldn't tame,
With a reputation that preceded her name.
But deep in the silence, beneath the facade,
Was a daughter who knew she was more than a fraud.

She didn't want the disappointment to stay,
Or to see the light in Mom's eyes fade away.
So she steadied her heart, she silenced the noise,
And traded the chaos for a quiet, steady poise.

While the world expected her spirit to break,
She proved them all wrong for her family's sake.
She walked across that stage, a win for the time,
The "bad kid" who made it, and finished her climb.

She knew she was better than the trouble she'd found,
More than the shadows that followed her round.
She wore her diploma like a badge of her soul:
A rebel who finally took back control.

HERITAGE

The kitchen was thick with the scent of the hearth,
Of cumin and chiles and the salt of the earth.
Mom stood at the stove while the iron was hot,
With a story and steam in every black pot.

Tacos and tamales, the food of our line,
To my young, hungry heart, it was sacred and fine.
But she sat apart with a different demand,
With a plate of fried chicken and bread in her hand.

The butter was thick and the crust was a gold,
A story of "American" flavors she told.
She'd push back the salsa, she'd turn from the spice,
Finding a world in the simple and nice.

I'd watch from my chair as she'd tear at the wing,
And wonder why she would ever eat that thing.
To turn from the heritage, rich and so deep,
For a bucket of take-out she wanted to keep.

She wanted the steak or the bread on the side,
While the rest of us swam in the Mexican tide.
Except for the night when the coals were all red,
And the scent of the carne would get in her head.

She'd reach for a tortilla, warm from the flame,
And butter it up as she called out its name.
A small, greasy bridge to the roots of our past,
In a meal that she finally wanted to last.

TABLE

The table was wide and the light was so low
The place where our stories were allowed to grow.
From homework to headers, from laughter to pride,
We gathered together with nowhere to hide.

I sat at the front, with my books and my pen,
In the warmth of a world that was safe for us then.
We didn't use filters, we didn't use masks,
We spoke of our days and our difficult tasks.

A "no-nonsense" ritual, honest and direct,
Where teasing was woven with threads of respect.
We'd poke at the armor, we'd laugh at the flaws,
Breaking the tension of all of life's laws.

I told them my heart, I told them my fears,
And they didn't just offer a bucket of tears.
They wouldn't say "right" or a "wrong" in the air,
They just showed me in silence that they were still there.

They listened to every word that we shared,
And answered in actions that showed they cared.
We grew up in jokes and in truth-telling songs,
In the family line where we all belonged.

No beating the bush or the secrets to keep,
Just a table of promises, heavy and deep.

BROWN BISCUIT

The turkey was carved and the steam was a cloud,
The table was bustling, the laughter was loud.
But the center of gravity shifted its weight,
To the very last biscuit left cold on a plate.

A golden-brown treasure, the final prize,
Reflected in four hungry, narrowing eyes.
Lizzy and I, we were locked in a stare,
A silent-movie tension that hung in the air.

No words were needed, no warnings were sent,
We both knew exactly where the fingers were bent.
I lunged for the bread with a hand fast and lean,
In the quickest maneuver that kitchen had seen.

But the silver flashed out like a strike from a snake,
A choice that a sister was willing to make.
The tines of the fork found the back of my hand,
A jagged, sharp map of the lines in the sand.

I looked at the metal, just hanging in place,
And looked at the smile on her satisfied face.
I screamed as the shock started turning to heat,
But I didn't let go of the bread or my seat.

The parents erupted in anger and dread,
While the fork dangled down from the prize I had fed.
The scolding was muffled, the details are blurred,
But the message was one that was clearly heard.

Forty years later, the mark is still there,
A small, silver ghost that I've chosen to wear.
A souvenir from a table of grit and of pride,
Where we fought for the biscuit with nowhere to hide.

SURGE

NEON

The driveway was quiet, the engine was low,
As we told them the places we wanted to go.
A movie, a mall, a friend's house nearby—
A soft-spoken, sisterly, foolproof lie.

But as soon as the taillights were out of their sight,
We turned toward the city and into the night.
From the safety of suburbs to the neon and glare,
Of Sunset and Hollywood, with smoke in the air.

West Hollywood beckoned with its electric hum,
The place where the rockers and outcasts would come.
We'd park on a side street and step to the curb,
Leaving behind every rule and proverb.

She walked like she owned every crack in the street,
With the rhythm of Hollywood under her feet.
I was the witness, the sister, the guard,
In a world that was glamorous, jagged, and hard.

We'd wander past clubs where the music was loud,
Lost in the swirl of a super cool crowd.
She wasn't allowed there without us in tow,
But she was the one with the spirit to go.

We were her cover, her "safe" little crew,
While she explored everything wild and new.
A secret we carried when we said goodbye—
The truth of the streets and the Hollywood lie.

PASSPORT

The stars were beneath us, names etched in the stone,
A map of the famous and the worlds they had known.
But I wasn't looking at the legends of old,
I was watching the glow turn the pavement to gold.

The air was a heavy, electric perfume—
Of exhaust and the nightlife that started to bloom.
I saw things I shouldn't—the dark and the wild,
The pulse of the city through the eyes of a child.

The smell of the cruising cars, steel and gasoline,
A dizzying, beautiful, Hollywood scene.
But the one thing that anchored the chaos for me,
Was the scent of the pizza we finally would see.

A dollar and fifty—a thin, greasy prize,
Reflected like magic in my hungry young eyes.
A hot slice of cheese and a cold can of Coke,
While around us the city's deep spirit awoke.

She'd buy it for me with a nod and a look,
A story not written in any "good" book.
The dirty street corners, the pizza-shop steam,
Walking the line of a Hollywood dream.

She was my passport, my guide through the glare,
With a slice in my hand and the night in our hair.
We stood on the names of the great and the dead,
While she made sure her sister was happy and fed.

THE YUKON

The clubs were off-limits, the doors were all barred,
To a sister too young for a world that was hard.
But the night didn't end when the music went still,
It moved to the Yukon on the side of the hill.

A twenty-four-hour refuge of light,
For the queens and the outcasts who owned the whole night.
I sat in the booth, mesmerized by the show,
In the scent of the coffee and the neon-lit glow.

They flowed through the doors in their glitter and lace,
With the sass of a goddess and paint on their face.
Empowered and loud, with a sting in their tongue,
The most beautiful creatures to a sister so young.

She sat there among them, her jacket pulled tight,
A butch kind of honor in the middle of night.
No sequins for her, just the leather and boots,
But they saw in her spirit the same kind of roots.

They'd talk for hours, they'd laugh and they'd tease,
While she navigated the shadows with ease.
I watched from the sidelines, the student, the guest,
Seeing a side of her put to the test.

She was cool with the queens, she was one of the crew,
A leader in places that nobody knew.
The Yukon was home when the sun started to rise—
A world of empowerment seen through my eyes.

CANOPY

The bus had left us at the edge of midnight,
Far from the comfort of a porch lamp's light.
The sky opened up in a sudden, cold pour,
As we walked down the street, a long asphalt floor.

Bassett stood silent on the right of the way,
A ghost of the school in the shadows of gray.
The rain was a deluge, a heavy, dark drum,
And the fear in my chest had started to hum.

A stranger was there, a few paces behind,
In the jagged, sharp logic of a teenager's mind.
The darkness was absolute, the sidewalk was slick,
And the pulse in my throat was starting to tick.

But she didn't panic, she didn't lose pace,
Though the water was running in streams down her face.
She reached for her jacket, the denim so worn,
The shield of a sister, the armor she'd sworn.

She pulled it from shoulders and cast it on high,
A canopy held between me and the sky.
"Stay calm," she whispered, her voice like a stone,
In a world that felt suddenly, dangerously lone.

We huddled together, two shapes in the storm,
Under the fabric that kept us both warm.
She was the anchor, she was the lead,
Moving with purpose and unshakable speed

I remember the drips on the tip of my nose,
And the scent of the jacket—or the cold of my toes.
The long, dark stretch of the Bassett High wall,
And the sister who wouldn't let anything fall.

We outran the shadow, we outpaced the fear,
Until the safety of home was finally near.
The door clicked behind us, the stranger was gone,
And we stood in the warmth till the coming of dawn.

NO 'STOPS'

The rules were unwritten, a family creed:
To never "technically" stop for our speed.
We'd approach every light with a slow, gentle roll,
Keeping the momentum and the car in control.

Mom at the wheel of the station wagon sled,
While the motorcycle's shadow was flickering ahead.
Allie was slick, with the metal and roar,
Looking for shortcuts and an open-sky door.

She saw the gas station, a gap in the line,
A calculated maneuver, a classic design.
She veered from the asphalt, she aimed for the win,
While Mom just stayed steady with a knowing, small grin.

What Allie had missed, but our mother had known,
Was the long, silver fence that the station had grown.
A chain-link barrier, a dead-end of steel,
That stopped the momentum of the heavy wheel.

She was blocked in the corner, a cat in a trap,
While we glided past her with a sarcastic clap.
I saw her shocked face as the wagon rolled by,
With the "No-Stops" laughter and the spark in her eye.

She wasn't defeated, it was clear and plain,
She was impressed by the master of the "shortcut" lane.
Mom didn't use lectures or a "tough woman" shout,
She just knew exactly what the race was about.

We made it to Tia Lucy's with a steady-set pace,
The victors of the "No-Stops" and the station-gate chase.
Even the sister had to bow to the view:
That Mom was the one who could always see through.

LEAN

The night was a velvet, cooling air,
With a hum of the engine and wind in my hair.
I'd watched her for years, a rider so bright,
And finally, I was the one in her sight.

I climbed on the back, my heart like a drum,
Waiting for the electric, sharp roar to come.
I was shy with my arms, I was hesitant and small,
Afraid of the balance, the speed, and the fall.

I reached for back handles, the metal and cold,
Instead of the sister I wanted to hold.
The engine erupted, a scream in the night,
As we launched from the curb and into flight.

But as the road curved and the asphalt would bend,
I fought with the gravity, world without end.
When she leaned to the left, I pulled to the right,
Countering her movement with all of my might.

I thought I was saving us, keeping us straight,
But I was the anvil, the mismatched weight.
She felt the resistance, the jerk of the machine,
The struggle of two on a seat in between.

"You have to move with me," she'd later declare,
"To stay with the rhythm and lean with the air."
But the ride was the only one I'd ever receive,
A memory of distance I couldn't quite leave.

I felt the disappointment, the sting of the "no,"
At the sister who traveled where I couldn't go.
I wanted to sync with her spirit and stride,
But I hadn't yet learned how to follow the ride.

SISTERS HOOD

Thunderbird stealth mode, a ghost on the block,
While the rhythm of tires was our only clock.
We were only a minute from the safety of her home,
In the weight of the white and the heavy-set dome.

But the quiet was broken, the evening disrupted,
By a stranger's anger, sudden and corrupted.
She didn't stay seated, she didn't stay still,
She stepped from the car with a steady-set will.

The man was a mountain, his temper was high,
Threatening the sister who owned the whole sky.
I watched from the seat as the tension grew deep,
A promise of violence he intended to keep.

But the door swung open, and then there were three,
My other sister and finally—me.
I didn't know the "why" or the "how" of the fight,
I only knew my sister was standing for might.

The "protected" one, the child, the guest—
Stepped out to put her own heart to the test.
We stood on the pavement, a line in the sand,
Ready to fight with the strength of our hand.

The man saw the fire, he saw the three-fold,
And the "tough" guy's bravado turned suddenly cold.
He retreated to shadows, he drove from the scene,
Afraid of the sisters and the space in between.

I realized then, in the Rowland glow,
That the "protected" one had started to grow.
I was ready to strike, I was ready to bleed,
For the sister who'd always been everything I'd need.

The roles had shifted, the circle was done—
Three sisters standing, together as one.

TRADE

The white car idled, a heavy-set weight,
Moving through blocks at a silent rate.
She steered through the shadows, steady and tight,
To manage the business in the middle of night.

I sat in the passenger seat, knowing the cost,
Of the secrets she carried and the lines that she crossed.
She had all the money, the treasures, the pull,
With a wallet of paper and a life that was full.

But the white, tiny bags were a heavy, dark weight,
A gamble with shadows and a bargain with fate.
She never touched what she traded away,
Keeping her own mind as clear as the day.

She was the dealer, the one with the key,
But she built a high wall between the business and me.
"Don't touch it," she'd warn, with a look like a knife,
"Don't ever let this kind of ghost take your life."

She wanted me safe, she wanted me pure,
While she navigated the sickness and cure.
It's a jagged, hard truth for a sister to hold:
That the hands that protected were buying the gold.

She was the tough one, the leader, the lead,
Sowing the harvest and the poisonous seed.
Yet she'd look at my face with a desperate pride,
And tuck all the darkness away deep inside.

A sister in denim, a ghost in the street,
With the rhythm of danger under her feet.
She was the silence and power all in one—
The "bad" girl who wanted her sister in the sun.

PERMIT

The house was a hive, a swarm of the bold,
With a permit in hand and a story to be told.
She'd sent out the word to the West Hollywood lights,
To the queens and the dreamers who owned the long nights.

I sat at the door with the box for the pay,
Counting the cover while the music would play.
Then the shadows appeared at the edge of the gate,
With the colors of gangs and a fearful fate.

Tough and intimidating, they stood with a stare,
With a weight in their stance and a solid look of a glare.
I stammered a warning, a "this isn't your kind,"
With the prejudiced logic of a narrow young mind.

"This isn't your preference," I whispered in fear,
Hoping they'd vanish or just disappear.
But the biggest one looked me right in the eye,
With a truth that I hadn't expected to fly.

"This is my preference," he said with a grin,
As he reached for his friend and he pulled him right in.
The cops hit the sirens, the blue and the red,
Trying to silence the words that were said.

But Allie had paperwork, a license for fun,
The keeper who'd thought of it all, one by one.
The house was a melting pot, packed to the door,
Of gangsters and drag queens on one single floor.

I learned in that moment, with the box in my lap,
That the world doesn't fit on a standardized map.
She trusted me there at the mouth of the cave,
To witness the different ways people are brave.

LONELY

I was the nurse in the small, quiet room,
Before I had learned how to flower and bloom.
With the needle and spirit, the water and soap,
I was the hands and the heartbeat of Hope.

At six, she had taught me the weight of a word,
With a slap that was felt and a lesson that stirred.
But after that moment, the anger was through—
She was witty and sharp, and she loved what I'd do.

I'd walk to the stove in the evening's low glare,
With a Kool 100 and the smoke in the air.
Menthol and fire, a spark on the tip,
Before I would hand it to her waiting lip.

I learned how to breathe in the silver and gray,
As I helped her navigate through every long day.
Nearly blind in her chair, with a leg that was gone,
I was the light she would lean herself on.

While Allie was chasing the distance and speed,
I was the one answering every small need.
She was the ghost who would come and would go,
While I was the breath in the steady and slow.

They say I was spoiled, the youngest of six,
Mainly ignored, a plan that was an easy nix.
But I was the lonely one, quiet and small,
The one with a sick mother to answer my call.

No one to brush through the knots in my hair,
Or teach me the secrets of what I should wear.
I went to the school with dirt on my clothes and skin,
With a hollow and heavy-set feeling within.

I didn't know freedom, I didn't know flight,
I only knew service in the middle of night.
She loved me, I knew it, in the way that she could,
In the "job" of a daughter that I understood.

But the mother I cared for, so funny and kind,
Was a mother who left her own daughter behind.
A keeper of secrets, a lighter of flames—
A life built of service and unspoken names.

GO

The door didn't slam, and the words weren't said,
As I followed the path where freedom led.
I didn't say goodbye, they didn't say stay,
I just let the silence carry me away.

Eighteen years of needles, eighteen years of smoke,
Under a caregiver's heavy, invisible yoke.
I reached for a friend and a different life,
Away from the illness, the struggle, the strife.

I feel the shame now, in the gray of my years,
Watering the past with these late-blooming tears.
I left her with Dad and the ghost of the hall,
While I ran from the duty, the debt, and the call.

A year later, she vanished, she slipped from the light,
Before I could tell her I'd made it all right.
Before I could say, "I'm sorry, I'm here,"
To wash away every old shadow and fear.

But the girl who walked out wasn't cruel or unkind,
She was just a child who'd been left far behind.
She didn't know how to be free and still stay,
So she chose the only and loneliest way.

I carried that weight like a stone in my chest,
Thinking I'd failed some impossible test.
But Mom knew the hands that had cared for her so—
She knew that the daughter she loved had to go.

GIFT

The house was dedicated to medicine and strain,
A quiet, slow rhythm of shadow and pain.
I'd left at eighteen to find my own way,
But the needs of the family called me back to the day.

With Allie and Lizzy, and Mom in her chair,
They built me a sanctuary, heavy and rare.
I was used to the "musts," the chores and the bread,
To the practical life where the family was fed.

But Mom reached for magic, for a different way,
The Game Boy I'd wanted for many a day.
The click of the buttons, the Tetris of old,
A treasure more precious than diamonds or gold.

I stood with my cake in the flicker and gleam,
While the house felt, for once, like a beautiful dream.
She looked at me then with a knowing, deep look,
A final, bright map that the memory took.

She died eight months later, the party was through,
But she gave me a piece of her heart to hold true.
I play the old game and I hear the same tune,
And I'm back in her arms in that late afternoon.

She gave me the "want" instead of the "must"—
The final, sweet "magic" between both of us.

I. DEPARTURE

The glass was liminal, a cold, thin line,
Between the dreaming and the shattering sign.
A shout from the pavement, a name in the dark,
Under the glow of a streetlight's spark.

I looked to the window, my heart in a blur,
Searching the shadows until I found her.
I saw her silhouette, short and so still,
A shadow of strength, a show of her will.

"Allie?" I whispered, my heart in my throat,
"Is it Mom?" and her "Yah" was the only note.
I stepped to the Thunderbird, white in the night,
Leaving the safety, as my chest got tight.

We drove in a silence that tasted of lead,
Through the empty streets where the unspoken was said.
Past Bassett, on the long, dark run,
Before the first glimmer of the morning sun.

Then the words finally fell, heavy and cold:
"Hope is gone." The debt was all told.
I screamed till the air was a shattered, sharp glass,
Watching the streetlights and the night-lights pass.

A blurred, electric world of shadow and gray,
As we raced toward the house where the silence would stay.
Two blocks away, through the mist and the gloom,
I saw the ambulance leaving its burden of doom.

No Hope in the sirens, no reason to fly—
Praying that this was all a lie.

II. THRESHOLD

The sidewalk was a cold, grey stone,
With the scent of wet grass and the hollow and lone.
I walked through the door to the wailing and cries,
To the tears of the aunts and the sorrowful sighs.

I was a ghost in the hallway, a heart turned to lead,
Moving through rooms where the world was now dead.
I stood at the door, at the edge of the frame,
Whispering a "sorry" and calling her name.

I watched for the rise of her stomach and chest,
Waiting for life to return from its rest.
A cruel little hope in the morning's dark sky,
Watching for movement, a ghost of a lie.

I stared from the distance, afraid to go near,
Caught in the static of shock and of fear.
While Lizzy was lost in her sobbing and cry,
Allie stood guard as the shadows went by.

They stood in the shadows, a line by the wall,
For the mother who'd been the heart of us all.
I stood at the line where the breathing had quit,
Accepting the truth, every piece of it

III. VOID

The world didn't shatter, it didn't go dark,
It just lost every meaning and every small spark.
I walked through the days like a ghost in the street,
With the rhythm of tequila and pavement and heat.

I didn't feel longing, I didn't feel pain,
I just wanted the nothingness to wash through my brain.
I was twenty and reckless, a wild, spinning wheel,
Searching for shadows so I wouldn't have to feel.

They said I was grieving, they said I was lost,
But I couldn't even calculate the cost.
There was no attachment, no tether or line,
To a mother whose life had been braided with mine.

I was the nurse who had outlived the task,
Hiding my hollow behind a drinker's mask.
I didn't think of her, I didn't see her face,
I just ran from the silence of the empty home space.

I was a nothingness moving through glitter and glare,
A sister in shadows who no longer did care.

ADRIFT

BOYSE

Behind the water machine, in the dust and the oil,
A Siamese stinker claimed a patch of the soil.
In a cardboard box with a Boise name,
He stepped from the shadows and rigged the game.

He wasn't just a stray, with fur of a ghost,
But a tiny dictator sucking up to his new host.
He'd climb up her leg—a jagged, sharp run—
Until he was perched in the heat of the sun.

On the shoulder of Allie, a throne made of skin,
He'd hammer those needles of acupuncture in.
She tolerated pain for the weight of the love,
A parlor-trick blessing from the blue eyes above.

We'd laugh at the sight, at the weird, funny ways,
Of a fur-covered gargoyle in a quiet space.
When Allie was gone, I was the one he would find,
With a blue-eyed devotion that was gentle and kind.

Ten years of magic, ten years of the claw,
Living by logic and Boyse's own law.

INVOICE

The house was a refuge, a steady-set place,
Where everyone found a safe, private space.
The girlfriend, the kids, the friends of the line—
They lived on her dollar, they lived on her time.

No worry for power, no worry for bread,
With a sister's bounty, the family was fed.
But I was the worker, the one with the bill,
A rent for the room and a test of the will.

Twenty and working, I searched for the pay,
While the others just drifted through every long day.
Why was I chosen to carry the weight,
In a house where the rest had a clean, open slate?

I stood on the corner when the shift was all through,
Waiting for headlights, for the sister I knew.
She promised a ride, she promised to come,
While the cold of the evening was making me numb.

But the white car was a ghost in the night—
She was late, she was missing, she was out of my sight.
The anger was quiet, a slow-burning flame,
At the sister who held me to a different game.

Was it love or a lesson? A push or a slight?
To leave me there waiting in the cooling street light?
She was the anchor for everyone else,
But she left me to find the strength in myself.

DUST

I. The Desk

The desk was a treasure, a drawer full of hidden,
Where the fragments of secrets stayed forbidden.
She'd warn me a thousand times—never to taste,
Never the shadow, the hunger, the waste.
But the air in the house was a heavy, dark lure,
I smoked the medicine, no longer pure.
I pinched at the dust in the wood and the grain,
Looking for something to silence the pain.

II. The Game

The guilt was a monster, a weight in my chest,
As I stepped from the house for a thirty-mile quest.
I fled to the city, to an ex's embrace,
Just to run from the look on my big sister's face.
We drifted in and out of smoke,
Lost in the grip of a desperate toke.
Gaming for days while my body wasted to thin,
Losing the world while the walls started in.

III. The Hall

In the quietest, loneliest time in Fall,
I was left in the chill of an ER hall.
With no name to give, and a ghost for a friend,
Waiting for how the story would end.
I carry the shame like a scar in my chest,
A ghost from a time I was put to the test

SCRATCH

The house was an oven of unspoken rage,
Fucking Allie—pacing a shadow-built cage.
The drugs she had traded, the powder and the dust,
Had finally swallowed the sisterly trust.

She was volatile, shifting like smoke in the air,
With a wildness in her eyes and a spike in her hair.
I reached for the phone, for a brotherly hand,
But she saw it—a line in the sand.

She lunged through the bedroom, a tempest of blows,
The end of the sisterly world that she knows.
Her ring dug deep in my eye and brow,
A mark of the "then" for the weight of the "now."

I fled to the corner, stunned and so blind,
Leaving the shattered, sharp wreckage behind.
The ambulance sirens, the white-walled scan,
The brutal results of the alexithymia plan.

A hematoma rose like a mountain of blue,
A barrier built between me and you.
To this very day, when the day starts to fade,
I see through the darkness the mark she made.

A scratch on the retina, a slightly dark veil,
A fragment of history, broken and frail.
The sister who carried me through the dark night,
Was the one who altered the way I see sight.

PATTERN

The distance was a desert, a year of hollow sand,
While I tried to understand the weight of her hand.
I lived in the "why," in the darkness of the blow,
Searching for a reason that a sister would go—

From the shield of my childhood to the storm in the hall,
To the shattered, sharp silence of the final, dark fall.
But now, in the quiet of the long look back,
I see the bruises and the jagged track.

It wasn't sudden, or a one-time spark,
But a pattern of power in the deep of the dark.
Her heavy rule was written in the sting,
A volatile, heavy, and complicated thing.

Then the news of the child came to soften the air,
And I reached through the static of the old, cold despair.
The violence retreated to the back of the mind,
As we left the hematoma and the anger behind.

But the scratch in my vision will always remain—
A ledger of love and a ledger of pain.

BLOOM

The news was a shiver of shock and of doubt,
A story the world couldn't quite figure out.
In her leather and boots, with her butch-hardened pride,
She had a secret that she no longer could hide.

The sister who moved like a man in the street,
Had a heartbeat inside that was steady and sweet.
The girlfriend was furious, angry, and cold,
In a broken-down story that wasn't yet told.

The sass and the power of the Hollywood nights,
Were lost in the hum of the hospital lights.
She struggled with the choice, with the weight of the "must,"
Trying to find something or someone to trust.

I watched from afar, with my husband and life,
Away from the drug-deals, the secrets, and strife.
She was closer to Lizzy, a separate road,
Carrying a new and heavy-set load.

She thought of the ending, she thought of the loss,
But she stood by the life and she weathered the cross.
The silent protector was taming her stride,
For the miracle growing and beating inside.

A butch kind of mother, a rebel with a child—
Finding the heartbeat that finally reconciled.

VALLEY

The white-walled halls of the Valley were bright,
As we gathered together in the fluorescent light.
The same cold floors where our mother would stay,
Now held a miracle, born on this day.

Dad and the girlfriend, Alex and me,
With Lizzy to guide her to what would be free.
She knew the shortcuts, the stamps, and the lines,
While I stood apart in my working-world designs.

Nik was a spark in a world made of steel,
A heartbeat of hope that was sudden and real.
No leather or armor could soften the blow,
Of a clinical truth that the doctors would know.

The drugs were in her system, the toxin was there,
A heavy-set shadow in the hospital air.
The girlfriend vanished, she fled from the door,
Leaving the sister alone for no more.

We gathered the pieces, we built a new way,
Through the darkness and dust of each passing day.
The shield of a sister, the mother of one—
A new kind of battle that had only begun.

SPLIT

We were sisters born of the same heavy house,
But I was the quiet, the working-world mouse.
While they chased shadows, the drugs, and the "game,"
I was building a different, more steady-set name.

They were masters of shortcuts, of "off-system" life,
Finding the loopholes through the struggle and strife.
I watched as Nik was raised in the "wild,"
A ghetto-taught lesson for a beautiful child.

Lizzy called me "uppity," she laughed at my pride,
Because I wouldn't cheat, or steal, or hide.
I loved them with honor, I guarded their truth,
Through all of the crimes of our volatile youth.

But Allie was different, a blur in the haze,
Just going through motions and navigating days.
She loved me, I knew it, in her shattered, sharp way,
Through the bitter and sweet of each passing day.

We were islands apart in a sea of the same,
Carrying the blood but a different kind of shame.

HEARTH

Her white Adidas would pull up to disturb,
A restless spirit that nothing could curb.
With a system in pursuit and a life on the wing,
Nik was a precious and heavy-set thing.

So they'd drop her with me, the sister of peace,
In a house where the shadows and fighting would cease.
I didn't have children of my own yet,
So I paid every tender and motherly debt.

I gave her the reach of a worker's own hand,
A softer-set peace she could understand.
My husband and I we built her a nest,
While the sister put her own heart to the test.

But "out of nowhere," her voice would roar,
And she would stand at the open door.
"I miss her," she'd say, with a look like a blade,
Taking back the safe home that we had made.

They'd vanish again in a sudden, sharp blur,
While we sat in the hollow and silence of her.
It broke us each time, the leaving and loss,
The heavy-set weight of a sister's cross.

She was never quite settled, she never was still,
A mother governed by an outlaw's will.
We were the safe house, the "uppity" shore,
Waiting for the sister to knock at the door.

REBEL IN PERSON

I had a refuge of silver and stone,
A place where the alternative world was my own.
Rebel In Person, my own sacred space,
With jewelry and clothing and a quiet, proud place.

Allie saw me standing on my own two feet,
And tried to help from her side of the street.
She sent a man, a family in tow,
A debt of honor she wanted to show.

I pierced the skin, I did the honest work,
But in their eyes, a jagged kind of smirk—
They walked through the door, away from the pay,
Taking the metal and the labor away.

I was shocked but not surprised by the slight,
By the outlaw logic in the middle of sight.
I called her up, my words heavy and cold,
At the "favor" she'd sent and the lies they had told.

She was upset, she felt the sting of the shame,
That her world and my world couldn't play the same game.
This little shop was a house made of law,
While hers was a world with a jagged-set flaw.

She wanted to give, she wanted to build,
But the well of her help was already filled—
With the thieves and the runners who knew her too well,
Turning my heaven to her own kind of hell.

AIR

The store was a sanctuary, a place of my own,
Where I'd reaped every harvest that I had ever sown.
But a shadow had entered and taken the prize,
Leaving distrust and fear in my working-world eyes.

Allie said she was sorry, the distance grew wide,
While she waited for justice and the turn of the tide.
Then came the phone call, a strange, quiet ask,
If we wanted an air conditioner to finish the task.

"It's free," she had whispered, "a gift for your home,"
With a look in her eyes that was hers alone.
I took it with thanks, I took it with care,
Not knowing the secrets that hung in the air.

Years later, the truth finally stepped from the dark:
She had waited for the sirens and the raiders to leave their mark.
When the handcuffs were clicked and the house was all still,
She moved through the shadows with a payback's will.

She took back the value, she took back the due,
To even the score for the sister she knew.
She gave me their treasures disguised as a gift,
The sister's maneuver, a complicated shift.

I laugh through the shock now, twenty years gone,
At the honor she carried from the dark to the dawn.
The sister who robbed for the sister who worked—
Where justice and loyalty no longer lurked.

SHALLOW

She was always a mountain, short and tall,
A Sovereign who wouldn't, and couldn't, fall.
But the drugs were a fog, a slow-drifting tide,
Where the sister I worshipped had started to hide.

She stayed in the shallows, she stayed on the rim,
While the light of her spirit was growing quite dim.
I reached for her often, I searched for the deep,
But she guarded the secrets she wanted to keep.

She told me the fractions, the small-talk, the lies,
With a wall of silence behind her dark eyes.
I was okay with the surface, the words that she'd lend,
Because diving deeper felt like the end.

I desperately wanted to pull her to land,
To offer my heart and to offer my hand.
To save the "Allie Cat" lost in the storm,
And bring back the rebel, steady and warm.

But she was a passenger, caught in the flow,
With secrets to keep and losing that glow.
She was still the strong sister, the one I once knew,
But addiction had built a wall that I couldn't get through.

I loved her in silence, I loved her from far,
Watching the light of my permanent star.

VESSEL

The Blue Chevy Nova was a vessel of hope,
A brother-in-law's gift—a steady-set rope.
But the drugs were a current, a pull of the tide,
That swallowed the motor and the cat's pride.

She vanished from the driver's seat, from the polish and glare,
To a shed in a backyard with dust in the air.
I felt for her then, the Ally Catt brought low,
With nowhere to turn and nowhere to go.

But she left me a miracle, a daughter to hold,
Whose future was vivid and still untold.
For five quiet years, in the warmth of our home,
Nik was safe from the streets where the shadows didn't roam.

We ironed the clothes, we brushed through the hair,
A level of loving that finally was there.
She thrived on the screen and she shone in the school,
Living a life by a beautiful rule.

While Allie was drifting and doing her own,
The seed of her daughter was peacefully grown.
I became the mother I wished I had known,
In a house with a heart that was steadily shown.

The sister was lost in the backyard of night,
But she gave me the chance to set a little girl right.

HOLLOW

The house was a sanctuary, steady and quiet,
A peaceful escape from her heavy riot.
For five beautiful years, she was ours to protect,
With a home of her own and a deep-set respect.

I gave her the world that I never had known,
A seed of the future that was peacefully grown.
Then Allie returned like a storm from the shed,
With a wild kind of logic inside of her head.

She wanted her daughter, her anchor, her pride,
To follow her on the next, jagged ride.
I felt the injustice, the anger, the dread,
At the responsible burden that I had to tread.

They looked at me then like a villain in wait,
As if stability was a reason for hate.
The youngest in line, with a voice never heard,
Dismissed by the brothers who honored the disturbed.

They loved the rebellion, the funny, the loud,
While I held the wreckage away from the crowd.
She stole her away in the middle of day,
With no word of goodbye as she carried the prey.

Pulled from school and the life we had built,
Leaving me drowning in sorrow and guilt.
Her toys were still there, her room was a ghost,
The final, sharp sting of the family's host.

It took years to see them, to cross through the line,
Between her wild world and the safety of mine.
I was the bad person for keeping things sane—
A lonely protector that stayed in her lane.

NIT

The white Adidas would drift back to my door,
Bringing the daughter I'd longed for and bore—
Not in my body, but deep in my soul,
Trying to keep her together and whole.

But each time she'd surface, my heart would just break,
At the heavy-set toll that the sister would take.
I counted the times—a tally of pain—
Nineteen long battles against the neglect and the stain.

With the fine-toothed comb and the sting of the soap,
I scrubbed through the tangles for a glimmer of hope.
While Allie was drifting, or fighting, or high,
The daughter was itching under a hollow-set eye.

Then came the "miracle," the trailer-park gate,
A narrow, thin room for a cat's fate.
"I'm clean," she would tell me, with eyes sharp and bright,
Searching for honor within my sight.

I waited and watched, with a wary-set mind,
Leaving the "Shed" and the shadows behind.
Nik went back to the world of the school,
Living again by a standardized rule.

I kept the comb ready, I kept the soap near,
For the next time the sister would just disappear.
I was the worker, the one with the home,
Trying to protect Nik from the urge to roam.

ECHO

The trailer park was a shadowed and musky place,
Where the smell of the smoke lived in every dark space.
I walked through the door to the damp and the mold,
A cramped, metal box that was starting to fold.

A single, small room for a mother and child,
Tucked in a city that was quiet and mild.
The school was a good one, the streets were all clear,
Away from the gangs and the old-fashioned fear.

But inside that box made of metal and tin,
The ghost of the street was starting within.
I saw it in Nik—the hyper-strong heart,
The rebel defiance is beginning to start.

She had that cold distance, looking for a fight,
A mirror of Allie in the darkest of night.
It scared me to see it, the cycle so near,
The rebellion returning in the face of my dear.

I brushed through her hair but I couldn't scrub out,
The spirit of Allie that was starting to sprout.

YOKE

She never wore a mask or hid behind a plea,
She owned the shattered mirror of the girl she used to be.
"I know the wrong I'm doing," she'd say with steady eyes,
Stripping away the layers of the standard, "sorry" lies.

She was honorable in wreckage, accountable and true,
Even as she walked the paths she knew she shouldn't do.
I was the stubborn sister, the one who wanted more,
Piling heavy expectations at her trailer-park door.

I fought her for the better, I fought her for the "best,"
While she was simply trying to pass a different test.
"I moved out of the shadows," she argued through the smoke,
"I found a better city and a lighter, easier yoke."

She had climbed from the backyard shed and left the dirt behind,
To give her daughter quiet and a sanctuary to find.
But I was blind to the distance she had traveled in the dark,
Only seeing where she faltered and where she missed the mark.

She respected that I stayed on the straight and steady shore,
Even as I demanded that she give me something more.
Looking back two decades, I see the cat's pride—
How much she had to battle just to turn the inward tide.

She was doing better, in her own fractured way,
Grateful for the trailer park at the ending of the day.

KIN

GRAVITY

I bought a house of my own in a tough and heavy town,
The only patch of earth where I could lay my head down.
She knew the streets were hard, she knew the shadows too,
But she stayed within the circle of the sister she knew.

Instead, she felt the pull, a magnet in the bone,
To move closer to the family she had always, deeply known.
She found a better city, just a few miles down the track,
Where the school was safe and she wouldn't have to look back.

Like a star following a moon, she shadowed every move,
Finding geographic comfort in the rhythm of sister-love.
She loved my children fiercely, she adored their little faces,
Finding refuge from the streets in our ordinary spaces.

I'd pick her up in my car, the shuttling of the years,
Washing out the distance and the volatile old fears.
We were building back the bridge, one drive and one debate,
Leaving the backyard shed to the shadows of the fate.

No longer miles apart in the ways we used to live,
We found something in the proximity we finally could give.

THE GIRL WHO CAME WITH THE HOUSE

We settled into Pomona, the fruit and the sun,
Temporarily leaving the ghosts of La Puente for a life that had begun.
The first day at the threshold, the boxes and the dust,
We met a little eleven-year-old finding a place to trust.

Tanya was a shadow with a kind and weary face,
Searching for warmth in a simple clean place.
"The girl who came with the house," Allie's laughter would roll,
As we offered her the WiFi and the peace of our soul.

We dressed her, we fed her, we shielded her from the "bad,"
Giving her the stability that her blood had never had.
She asked if we needed help, sweet and eager to please,
As she finally found a refuge and rested with ease.

Thirteen was the custody, sixteen was the name,
A different kind of family that no longer felt the same.
From the streets of the homeless, to the lab and the degree,
A molecular scientist, Zelda shining and free.

Allie witnessed the triumph, the honor, and the rise,
With a secret kind of wonder behind her quiet eyes.

MELTING

Fifteen years of waiting in a quiet, empty hall,
Before the miracle of Sebby came little and small.
Her eyes were shining, a Godmother-now-made,
In a house where the loneliness had finally started to fade.

Allie, with her quiet ways and steady, private pride,
Step by step she moved to let the children's world inside.
She wasn't one for easy smiles or making any show,
But carried a deeper kind of love that only we would know.

But when she held her Kitty, when she held the third one too,
A softness in her spirit was finally breaking through.
She spoiled them with treasures, with toys and gifts of gold,
A history of "don't ask" that neither of us told.

"Did you pay for this?" I'd whisper, afraid of what I'd find,
Searching for the truth in the corners of her mind.
She'd answer with a "Yes" and that sly, knowing smile—
Her own kind of magic in a sisterly style.

A look that confessed what we both knew was true,
That she'd pay any price just to carry them through.
She traded the facts for the peace in our walls,
The guardian of "yes" whenever they'd call.

A sister's gift wrapped in secrets and in pride,
With nothing but the heartbeat of Allie Cat inside.

KITTY-KITTY

The first of the month was a goody feast,
When the worries of money were quiet and least.
With $40 tucked into her wallet fold,
She bought them the magic that couldn't be sold.

KFC buckets and Dollar Store runs,
For the Meow-Meow and Kitty-Kitty, her favorite Godsons.
"Pick ten," she would whisper with a wide, sneaky grin,
Letting the thrill of the choosing begin.

She'd steer her scooter to Chris's for cream,
A chocolate scoop, a flicker of a child's dream.
She didn't need riches to build them a day—
She was the fairy godmother to show them the way.

I'd panic at the sight of the six-year-old hands,
On the wheel of her car in the suburban lands.
"Drive it," she'd laugh as they sat on her lap,
A wild kind of lesson with no kind of map.

They were flying, they were daring, they were children of speed,
Finding the fire for everything they'd need.
"If anyone messes," she'd vow with a spark,
"I'll handle it," guarding them there in the dark.

No bank could record it, no ledger could hold,
A sisterly love, more precious than gold.

AIM

The toy store aisles were a maze of the bright,
Under the hum of the fluorescent light.
She walked with the boys, her grumpy, hard shell
Hiding the heaven she wanted to tell.

A rebel on a mission, a girl with a cause,
Rewriting the script of all childhood laws.
"Pick anything," she'd whisper with a nod and a look,
Giving them magic not found in a book.

Whatever they pointed to, whatever was shown,
She'd steady her aim and have them make it their own.
I stood in her shadow, worried and small,
Watching her presence take charge of it all.

She saved for the months and she handed me the pay,
To keep for the children on their special, bright day.
Even at one, or at two, when the concept was new,
The wealth was a symbol of the love that she knew.

A sister's own truth and a sly, knowing grin—
Buying them anything from the store within.
I wasn't allowed to ask or question the code,
I simply followed the path on her road.

Respecting the older, the rebel, the lead,
As she planted the seeds for everything they'd need.
The boys loved the magic, the gifts and the chase—
Kitty-Kitty's honor in a toy-cluttered space.

LEDGER

The miles to La Puente were a heavy-set road,
But the pull of the sister was a sacred-set code.
She needed a vessel, a way to get round,
To navigate the streets and the newfound ground.

I bought her the van, twenty-eight hundred strong,
A gift from a heart where she'd always belonged.
But the Sovereign hated the "handout" and "slight,"
She wanted the balance to be perfectly right.

She saw the world taking and draining my well,
And she vowed that she wouldn't be part of that hell.
"Fifty a month," she decreed with her pride,
The older sister honor she carried inside.

I took the crumpled bills and I made them her own,
The heaviest currency I had ever known.
It was restitution, a debt she had grown,
To settle the seeds of the life she had sown.

But I secretly circled the money back round,
In groceries and dinners and shoes for the ground.
I gave to be loved, I gave for the "Yes,"
In a desperate, younger-girl loneliness.

But Allie Cat knew, and she shielded my name,
Refusing to play in the "advantage" game.
She was the debt-payer, the fierce and the true,
Building a bridge with love that carried me through

TETHER

But soon, inflamed bronchi were traded for a vessel of air,
As the heavy-set years and the wear and the tear
Started to catch her and pull at her stride—
A Sovereign's body with nowhere to hide.

She needed the oxygen, steady and slow,
A new kind of engine for nowhere to go.
She found a room with a ghost from my past,
A friendship of decades that couldn't quite last.

An ugly and angry and bitter-set soul,
Who wanted power and wanted control.
I'd stepped from that circle, I'd stepped from the glare,
Leaving the sharp, jagged words in the air.

But Allie was different, she walked her own way,
Unbothered by grudges or the things people say.
She rented that room, she settled her weight,
Just a mile from my window and the La Puente gate.

It was strange and was awkward, a complicated line,
To have my old frenemy and the sister of mine—
Dividing the space while the Sovereign Cat
Anchored herself for a long, quiet chat.

She was liberated by the freedom of four wheels,
But tied to the tank and the way the heart feels.
A mile of distance was all that remained,
Between me and the Sovereign, both weathered and strained.

She chose the dark room just to be within reach,
Of the lessons of love only sisters can teach.

HAVEN

Seven years of living in a house made of stone,
In a room that she hated, bitter and lone.
She spoke of the "friend" with a jagged-set tongue,
An echo of anger from when we were young.

"Don't come inside," was her Sovereign's decree,
To guard the clean world she wanted for me.
I'd pull to the curb and honk at the gate,
Watching the door where the shadows would wait.

She'd step to the sidewalk, heavy and slow,
With nowhere but my passenger seat left to go.
Her breath was a struggle, her stride was a chore,
But she escaped through the opening of the passenger door.

"Turn up the AC," she'd gently demand,
As we drifted away from that "friend's" jagged land.
To errands and groceries, to miles and to chats,
The final, sweet kingdom of our Allie Cats.

I ached for her tired and weary-set soul,
Wishing my house could be made more than whole.
But the rooms were all filled, the space was all gone,
I carried the guilt from the dark to the dawn.

I couldn't bring her home to my full, busy life,
Leaving her there in the hollow and strife.
But inside the car, in the cool and the white,
We were the only things finally right.

NOCTURNE

We finally found the steady, even beat,
A sisterhood forged on a quieter street.
But the Sovereign's father, old and so kind,
Was drifting away in the haze of the mind.

He'd show up at eleven, a ghost in the drive,
With instruments ready to feel more alive.
On the patio floor, under the stars and the night,
He'd play for the children in the low-burning light.

The bottles were gone, the anger was still,
Replaced by the music and a different high will.
The grandchildren would dance, the laughter would roll,
A grandfather's blessing for every small soul.

But foreshadowed in silver, the warnings were there,
In the scrapes on the curb and the curving of air.
A mailbox leaning, a fender-set dent,
Quiet messages that the universe sent.

His driving was off, his vision was blurred,
By a symphony rising that neither had heard.
Allie and I, we watched through the glass,
As the shadow of time was starting to pass.

He was the man of the strings, fun and free,
But we knew he was drifting away from the family.
The rhythm was changing, the song was almost through—
A secret kind of sorrow, his mind had flew.

CYCLE

At fifty-eight, with the memories and ink,
With a lifetime of reasons to pause and to think,
The Allie Cat with the sharp, private claws,
Still bowed to the weight of her childhood laws.

She'd speak of the bruises, the anger, the dread,
Of the "child of the streets" and the words that he said.
But when she would call him, the years would all fall,
And "Daddy" was still the name she would call.

A paradox living in one weary breath:
Love and a loathing that lasted till death.
She knew she was "trouble," a storm in his sight,
The daughter who kept him awake through the night.

But shadows have habits of following feet,
And the cycles of anger are bitter and sweet.
The hand that was raised in the house of her youth,
Found its way to her own—a jagged, hard truth.

She carried the fire that had burned in his chest,
And passed on the spark that had put her to test.
She loved with a fierceness that sometimes would sting,
A sister's own rule is a complicated thing.

She wanted the honor, she wanted the light,
But she grappled with ghosts in the middle of night.
A "Daddy's girl" broken, a mother who tried,
With a fierce-beating heart and a storm kept inside.

BETRAYAL

The table where we spoke the truth is shattered into dust,
Betrayed by blood and legal ink and shattered, hollow trust.
They saw the shadow in his eyes, the flicker in his hand,
And moved like vultures circling to claim his kingdom's land.

A diagnosis of the slow, a quiet, creeping thief,
Became the weapon they would use to sharpen all our grief.
They spoke of "care" and spoke of "love" while counting out the gold,
Before the story of his life was even fully told.

We were blindsided, treated like the children in the yard,
By older brothers playing every jagged, legal card.
They sold the porch where music played, the walls where he was free,
And locked away the Sovereign from Allie and from me.

He begs us through the telephone, a broken, haunting plea:
"Please save me from this place and take me home and let me be."
But the house is gone, the keys are turned, the memories are sold,
To satisfy the brothers and the lies they've bought and told.

We stay away for mercy's sake, to dull the sharp-set pain,
Because seeing him and leaving him is more than he can strain.
I haven't spoken to them now in years of bitter rain,
The bridge they burned will never bridge the family again.

They took the father's dignity, they took the Sovereign's crown,
And watched the sisters' spirits simply, slowly drown.
Allie stood beside me in the shadow of the door,
Unified in fury and in something even more:

A dedicated kind of loyalty, forged in the same old fire—
Against the brothers' treachery and the greedy, dark desire.

02

The tank was heavy, and the breath was hard to find,
But she never left a single person behind.
A quiet kind of Cat, a tether to the air,
She'd drop the world just to show she was there.

She spoiled my boys and she loved on my girl,
The most precious treasures in her private world.
It didn't matter if her lungs were weary and slow,
If I needed her standing, she was ready to go.

We had our seasons of darkness and of deep,
Of promises we've broken and secrets we still keep.
But in the end, when the truth was laid bare,
She was the only one who was always, always there.

She taught me that honor isn't found in a name,
But in the sister who stayed through the trouble and the shame.
Though the oxygen hissed and the struggle was great,
She drew in her breath and she challenged her fate.

BROKEN

She was the wild card they feared in the dark,
A fire-starter with a deadly-set spark.
They knew of the "business," the price and the trade,
The Sovereign's history and the moves she had made.

But they saw her weakened, they saw her as frail,
And moved for the father while she was faltering and pale.
She went to the house, with a wicked-set tongue,
Fighting the battles that began when they were young.

A clash of the brothers, a yelling of hate,
While Dad sat in silence at the edge of the gate.
Horrible echoes, a shattering sound,
As the honor of family sank into the ground.

Then she came to my doorway, shocked and in pain,
A Sovereign retreating with nothing to gain.
I didn't know of the heart that was starting to break,
Or the heavy, dark toll that a brother could take.

The weight of the years and the brotherly sting—
A literal heartache that changed everything.
She wept in my arms, a lifetime in a blur,
Releasing the secrets that were buried in her.

The tough-woman armor was laid on the floor,
As Allie Cat cried like she couldn't no more.
She knew she was fading, she knew of the end,
With a father to mourn and a break she couldn't mend.

VOYAGE

The white van was a memory, a phantom of no speed,
Replaced by a scooter for her every slow need.
I sensed the shift, the shadow, the quiet, dark tide,
But denial was a curtain where I wanted to hide.

I needed to wash the horribleness from her soul,
To take back the fragments and make her feel whole.
So we aimed for Alaska, for the glaciers and blue,
Her lifelong dream that only a few knew.

Ten days on the water, tanks and meds in tow,
A feline on a voyage with nowhere to go but "go."
She wheeled her scooter through the streets of the North,
Calling her freedom and her dignity forth.

We panned for the "shimmer" in the cold, rushing stream,
A sparkle of truth in a flickering dream.
We ate at the salmon-bake, the smoke in the air,
With nothing but joy and the wind in our hair.

I watched her face brighten as she stared at the sea,
A gift of the "possible" for her and for me.
We stood for the lens, for the portrait of grace,
A sisterly bond in a limitless space.

It is the breath of the North that I carry today:
The look on her face before we drifted away.
Her wishes were met in the wild and the vast—
The peace of the water, at long, long last.

MERCY

The Alaskan air was a sharp, cold gift,
A moment of mercy, a weightless lift.
We sat on the deck as the ship turned for home,
Watching the churn of the white and the foam.

She looked at the water, so endless and deep,
With a secret of peace she was ready to keep.
The grumpy exterior had softened to gold,
In a story of sisters that finally was told.

"I made it," she whispered through tanks and the mist,
Counting the miracles that still could exist.
The anger of brothers, the sting of the shed,
Were lost in the glaciers and the words we had said.

But the rhythm was slowing, I felt it in me,
The Sovereign was tethered and bound to the sea.
We returned to the heat of the La Puente street,
With the salt on our skin and the trip complete.

She gave me her hand, she gave me her pride—
The last of the "Allie Cat" living inside.

HEART

The gold was still bright in our mind,
But the shadows of home were waiting to find—
The daughters of sorrow, the broken and lone,
Watching the brothers set their own tone.

Allie wanted the truth to be shouted and told,
Before the final, dark silence was allowed to take hold.
She planned for the visits, the door-to-door plea,
To expose the betrayal to the whole family tree.

But her breath was a ghost, her strength was a thread,
And faith started flickering inside of her head.
She went to the facility, weary and slow,
To regulate life in her low-burning glow.

Then the readings spoke what her heart already knew:
Attacks in the silence, both old and many new.
I stood in shock—how was she still here?
Fighting the monsters, the shadows, and fear.

I felt hopeless and hollow, a child in the rain,
Wishing my sister could be free from the strain.
But the Sovereign was stubborn, her will was a wall,
Refusing the mercy of the final, dark call.

She carried the heartache, the betrayal and cost,
Guarding the pieces that hadn't been lost.
Splintered but standing, silent and tough—
Because being her sister was finally enough

ALLIE-NESE

She looked at me and asked for a sister's guarantee,
"Be my voice," she whispered with a heavy-set decree,
Handing me the keys to the things she couldn't be.

In her youth, she used her knuckles, she used her fist and fire,
The only way a fighter knew how to climb higher.
But she admired how I spoke, the way I'd explain,
The untangling of beauty and the untangling of pain.

She called me "smart," a title I had never dared to claim,
While I held her on a pedestal and guarded her great name.
I kept her on a pedestal, a figure etched and crowned,
The warrior who shielded me and kept my feet on the ground.

And she stood on her own pedestal, looking down at me,
At the sister with the language to set the spirit free.
We were mirrors for each other, complicated and deep,
With promises of Allie-nese that we finally could keep.

I am speaking for the Sovereign, I am speaking for the Cat,
In the vulnerability of silence where the two of us once sat.
She trusted me to tell it, to find the perfect word,
So the story of her honor could be finally, truly heard.

CAT GONE HOME.

The phone was a shattering, low-set sound,
As the world I had known sank into the ground.
"Tita," she whispered, scared and so small,
"I can't wake her up; she won't answer at all."

I raced through the rain, from the city to her home,
Under the grey of the sky and the rusty chrome.
But there at the curb, the world was a still, wet frame—
My husband, my child—silencing her name.

Beneath an umbrella, they stood in the street,
With looks of finality, cold and complete.
Their eyes were reflectors of the grief in the air,
Static and silent, just waiting there.

I walked through the doorway, numb and so still,
To the room where my sister had bowed to God's will.
She lay on her chair, in the way that she slept,
While around her the silence shuddered and wept.

I reached for her then, in the musky-set gloom,
The same way she held me in The Brown Van's room.
The first time, the last time—the weight was the same,
A sisterly anchor, her shield for my flame.

I cradled her head as the rain hit the glass,
Waiting for the last of her spirit to pass.
I closed the dark door, I sat for a while,
Searching her face for the "sly," knowing smile.

"Goodbye, Allie," I whispered with clouded sight,
Leaving the silence to cover her last fight.
The shield of my childhood was finally at rest,
With nothing but honor inside of my chest.

ABOUT THE AUTHOR

Herlinda is a lifelong creator with a gift for seeing beauty in places others overlook. After twenty-five years in the fashion industry, she learned how to rebuild, reimagine, and restore—skills she now brings to her writing. Rooted in faith, family, and the stories that shaped her, she writes as a mother of three and as a sister who finally found her voice. She lives in La Puente, California, with her husband of nearly three decades. The Sovereign Cat is her debut collection, born from a journey of healing, truth, and rediscovered voice.

www.ingramcontent.com/pod-product-compliance
Lightning Source LLC
Chambersburg PA
CBHW030054110726
47973CB00002B/24